Paul Hoover

Totem and Shadow: New and Selected Poems

by Paul Hoover

POETRY

Letter to Einstein Beginning Dear Albert (1979)
Somebody Talks a Lot (1983)
Nervous Songs (1986)
Idea (1987)
The Novel (1990)
Viridian (1997)
Totem and Shadow (1999)

FICTION

Saigon, Illinois (1988)

EDITOR

New American Writing (1986 to present)
Postmodern American Poetry: A Norton Anthology (1994)

Totem and Shadow
New and Selected Poems

Paul Hoover

Talisman House, Publishers
Jersey City, New Jersey

Published in the United States of America by
Talisman House, Publishers
P.O. Box 3157
Jersey City, NJ 07303-3157

Manufactured in the United Sates of America
Printed on acid-free paper

The cover drawing is used
by kind permission of the artist, Ian Robinson

• "Long History of the Short Poem," "Compared to What,"
"Tribal Item," "The Orphanage Florist," "Heart of Darkness,"
and "Sunlight in Vermont" are reprinted from
Paul Hoover, *Idea* (The Figures, 1987).
Reprinted by permission of the publisher.
• Chapters 24, 25, 30 by Paul Hoover, from
THE NOVEL.Copyright © 1990 by Paul Hoover.
Reprinted by permission of New Directions Publishing Corp.
• "In a Shadow Gate," "Stationary Journey," "Red Lilies,"
"Baseball," "Voices Off," "Night of the Hunter," "Desire,"
"The German Version," "Impossible Object," "As Quietly as Distant,"
and "The Garden" are reprinted from
Paul Hoover, *Viridian* (The University of Georgia Press, 1997).
Reprinted by permission of the publisher.

CONTENTS

New Poems

Viridian (1997)

The Novel (1990)

Idea (1987)

Nervous Songs (1986)

Somebody Talks a Lot (1983)

Letter to Einstein Beginning Dear Albert (1979)

ACKNOWLEDGMENTS

The author would like to thank Richard Friedman, Darlene Pearlstein, Art Lange, and Peter Kostakis of The Yellow Press, publisher of *Letter to Einstein Beginning Dear Albert*, 1979, and *Somebody Talks a Lot*, 1983; Bob McNamara and Bridget Culligan of L'Epervier Press, publisher of *Nervous Songs*, 1986; Geoffrey Young of The Figures, publisher of *Idea*, 1987; James Laughlin of New Directions, publisher of *The Novel*, 1990; and Bin Ramke, editor of the Contemporary Poetry Series of The University of Georgia Press, publisher of *Viridian*, 1997.

Section 25 of *The Novel* was reprinted in *The Best American Poetry 1989*, edited by Donald Hall and David Lehman. "Desire" was included in *The Best American Poetry 1991*, edited by Mark Strand and David Lehman. "Theory" was published in *The Best American Poetry 1993* edited by Louise Gluck and David Lehman. "Baseball" appeared in *The Best American Poetry 1994*, edited by A. L. Ammons and David Lehman. "As Quietly as Distant" was published in *20th Century Goodbye*, edited by Andrei Codrescu.

Grateful acknowledgment is made to the editors of the following publications, in which new poems have appeared: *American Poetry Review*: "Reflection's Edge," "Canticus Narcissus," "Totem and Shadow," and "In the Landing Zone"; *Triquarterly*: "Family Romance"; *Volt*: "Surface Gods"; *Salt* (Australia): "Local Knowledge"; *Green Mountains Review*: "Totem and Shadow"; *Common Knowledge*: "The System" and "In the Landing Zone"; *Columbia Poetry Review*: "In Which City"; *Jacket* (Australia): "Family Romance"; *Boston Book Review*: "At Unrest."

Totem and Shadow

New and Selected Poems

NEW POEMS

LOCAL KNOWLEDGE

They float; they
mean. Ripping their
there. What reaches

them, what smother?
Expected. . .seems to
lean as every

other voice soaking
in its moan,
its name and

evening pronounced as
words, vocables flashing
back—here, where

she's expected—like
refinement & forgiveness.
Throughout her head,

petroglyphs of sand
are crazed with
faults. Recent evidence,

local knowledge, like
light on faces
(gone again, due)

her first glance
takes. Not ripe
things seen. Thimble

in heaven. Van
Gogh's thousands of
grey-greens competing

for the landscape
because the mind
moves over it

like a hand.
Insistent sound of
keys turning in

locks, ice easing
down rivers, collard
green squeak. These

are memory's freaks,
the past breathing
back. Overadorned

and catastrophic, nature
takes serial journeys
past historic sites.

Hatched in water,
pinched life stirs.
As Emerson writes,

"Under every deep
a lower deep
opens." Not now,

but soon enough
and in language
one succumbs to

the cold mind's
warmth, immune to
praise, pitiless as

Paul Hoover

blame, having arrived
on different trains
and leaving each

by each. There's
no "new meaning."
Old worlds circle

beyond our contriving
yet with such
flavor the living

gods are flattered
back into their
graves. Balance means

cancel. They float,
they mean. Apparent
in their fervor.

TOTEM AND SHADOW

In Thicket Portage,
near the Arctic Circle,

the ground is frozen
all year long. White-

haired men drive white
buses across blue tundra.

The world, meanwhile,
is useful and social,

a weightless space
consisting of triumph,

waste, and desire,
which of course is

history, the dream
without the tangle.

Flocked like houses
in the squall of being,

events are dressed for
mourning everywhere we are.

Moralists at the boundary
of flesh and being,

we watch each generation
fold back into itself

like an urgent letter
that's finally never sent.

Paul Hoover

Covered with a snow
tainted and actual,

though not in fact real,
the concept of history

survives as a totem.
Cartoon graphics and

the Lascaux caves
emerge as the old.

We circle their shards
in the postmodern town,

our saliva and semen
dangerous as machines.

A hawkmoth drifts
toward a wintry aviary.

A width of crows
sways in thistles.

The world as act
is nimble as a shadow,

but we haven't
even the language

to speak its name.
Because the TV's on,

we can only watch intently
as the word *bruise*

darkens and the word
light brightens.

This is the way it is,
the present seems to argue:

a group of smiling firemen
posing in front of the fire,

an apocalypse so boring
its sequel is in planning.

THE SYSTEM

Here where belief
starves for attention,
The future is designed

by Michael Jackson.
Cartoon static blows
past the stars.

Even the cosmos
sits down loudly
to watch a show.

The actual lies
between two stations,
a ball of inertia

constructed from
the news. Authentic
as the past, the

dark marking silence
is wide as a giant.
Tossed in hours

and vanishing lamps,
this is snow's
district, personal as

a system, where
the book of
nerves will not

be written, its
light soft letters
composed as worlds.

Even the wind
enters velocity darkly,
moving in circles,

losing its way.
Public as desire,
uniform knowledge

leads to the cages.
The lexical evidence
ripens, shadow on

shadow. Time will
not unfold. Among
stone chats, things

are left unsaid:
the pike in
its pool, nobody

in bed. At
the lake garden's
gate, the evening

is weighing, its
small hill silver,
green trees wet,

and patterns of
cattle scattered like
ashes. Named at

night, misshapen by
saying, you sleep
magnified in western

darkness like
John Runk's boards.
Sharp in the mind,

your chalk outline
fits like a
glove. The church

field is brown,
sunshine in order.
Behind those walls,

the landscape of
a final country
surpasses all doors.

IN WHICH CITY

Radiant darkness,
collapsing light,

the full
catastrophe blurred—

tunnels under
worlds, another

lifeboat scene,
the present

absence felt
like mind's

named things.
In sequences

like smoke,
in deadbolt

light, your
father's back

is turned
against the

camera as
he faces

that field.
Words and

silence are
uttered like

a surface,
porous but

smooth. Like
when your

daughter's friend
says she

must decide
between her

father and
lover. Haven't

you purely,
places in

the leaves?
Falling too

darkly toward
that mouth?

Trembling like
a _____?

Note by
note, we're

mastered by
the shape

each wave
makes, since

what rises
rarely falls

exactly as
the getting.

Like an
anvil on

the table
teetering toward

the brink,
the language

of height
breaks with

weight. Each
act is

magic black
as space.

Moral darkness,
anonymous rot.

You live
transparent, the

ghost of
a chance

the light
inch spreads

to enter
its name.

FAMILY ROMANCE

You like
showing photos

blind as
light, decades

ripped to
shreds and

littered in
an album.

The future
is present

in history's
window, where

the brief
green world

observes its
turning. An

apple is
yellow at

the edge
of red.

In the
pallor of

the storm,
someone is

rouged in
distance. Your

mother and
father just

after marriage
smile at

the light,
their eyes

dark as
a harvest.

Form is
deep in

portions your
whole life

long—no
winter shadow

thin as
sin, just

broken stones,
a tottering

ghost. Ragged
as pleasure,

rain stabs
water. A

lighthouse on
the prairie

does no
less. What

is life,
what world

born five
miles back?

The *this*,
the whole

boat. When
your heart

is beating
and the

porch is
soaked, you're

drowning in
arousal and

always in
the frame.

AT UNREST

Since the green
familiar world

is everywhere present,
comfortable with

profusion and
lucky in crime,

I listen all day
to Miles Davis play,

beautifully and
clearly, "So Near,

So Far." In what
minor key is

beauty so muted
and icy as

the mind? Its
knock and shine

are trenchant as
an edge—all

the new thinking
in miniature

and in grandeur.
Shall I tell

my children
I heard today,

indulging madness
sweetly, the smoke

of heaven? The
future of memory

awaits no further
news. Diffusion

is a prayer
decided by ear

in honor of
my weakness.

Trouble and
desire are

at the lips
of stasis.

The sound
street rises.

THEORETICAL PEOPLE
for Maxine

Pervasive and
strange, love's

singular language
has ten

tongues. The
actual present

is blessed
with traffic,

intense bits
of emotional

baggage constant
as genres.

In memory's
rite, *I*

love, you
love is

all love's
yielding, to

cast our
shadows, cold

to cold,
on that

bright bed.
All our

histories fly
over a

white horizon
into a

patch of
park where

swell turns
dark. The

mind's ripe
distance is

transparent as
an edge.

We come
from afar.

That's that
then. The

map maker's
colors denote

no place
where the

sting of
love isn't.

Beyond all
resemblance, be

for me
the question.

REFLECTION'S EDGE

Like transforming engines,
their voices are loud,
and the things they say

are painful as stigmata.
When the freak storm
passes, they sit in silence,

amused by their weakness,
impatient with strength.
Secret and tragic,

the "empire of feeling"
is plausible as a riot.
They turn to the practice

of money, which cleanses
and endures. On that
shining track, hope

stands alone, half seer,
half crone. Applause
at the abdication.

Weeping at the ascension.
She is the stained bride
who penetrates marriage

with discipline and
and a knife. But poverty
breaks the pillow;

history is a mother;
redemption writes novels.
She has been transparent,

and he has been stone
in a strict provincial
world. Overgrown

with glamor, here is
the edge of pain,
and here is appetite

in three long pages:
father in a nursing home
crying in the wall,

their children folded
into their lives
like misplaced parcels.

Love burns, and
from those ashes
disaster's new longing

scratches up through snow.
Bereft as a witch, she waits
for something deadly,

but nothing real happens
and even the ghosts know.
Inspections and tribunals

leave nothing to desire,
everything reduced
to a hedgerow calm,

the light in their eyes
dark as the window.
Structures in the fog

disappear like ships.
Angled in the glass,
Guatemala wobbles.

SURFACE GODS

"On the edge of no cliff" —Jack Spicer

With no secret place
and no unveiling,
the word is round

for whom the public ripens—
a generation spoken,
your own game face.

Pharaonic. Sweet.
Eternity's black thread
raveled too tightly.

The cost isn't language
translated into acts
but virile architecture

familar as Jack—
bloated and sick—
singing in depression.

To love and fail,
furious to the root,
is life as it turns.

A modernist pagoda
on a futurist lawn,
indelible stumble

toward some right field,
the circumstance and glamor
of passing back out.

Formed as voices,
outside the outside,
we have one language

Paul Hoover

and counting down.
Syllables of madness.
Faith's ten towns.

The mouth as it speaks
twisted in belief,
distances adrift in

"white and aimless signals."
Not the thing itself
but a diagram of the harvest.

CANTICUS NARCISSUS

Behind the body of a suicide blond,
the theory of resurrection,
which is only, of course, a theory
but causes bodies to rise and float
like thin magician's assistants.

Behind each object, its universal shadow,
ancient shapes with no traditions
but a history of being.

Behind the storm, a freezing,
behind each death, two lives.
Behind the eye, an image as the mind
insists on having it seen,
mother for instance lying near death
with rouged cheeks the nurse applied.

Behind your desire, the starkness of the world.
Behind each ghost, eagerness and hunger.

Behind the news that can't be printed,
a cold rain falling, for this is not the world,
and this is not the dark. This is the word as mark,
where high in the attic of introspection
you can smell the chimichanga.

Before the thought, the sign; before the mouth, a name.
The world begins with the intimacy of distance
and ends with a crowding. It is then (then)
when (when) terrible and terrible
we are enamored of the sheer work of existence,
abstract meetings of flesh and flesh.

Instead of the age, a falling;
before the sheet, the winding.

Fat with winter, which here means rain,
we are on a future street. The sound of wheels
must mean: tusk of waking, birth of a pearl,
storm over park, rim shot timing.

On a hill overlooking a world,
these are the homes of the shining.

IN THE LANDING ZONE

Where the proud and the vacant
don't live up to their names,

where the unconscious hammers
inside a clean cupboard,

where civic is ironic
and a salesman's shadow burns,

where you lie in the shards
of the metaphors of the age,

citizen of a place
yet to be discovered

but soon to be replete,
where the signs are lovely and sleepy

beneath their neon paint,
where life is as unexpected

as a horse eating a sandwich
and all the architecture

is one inch out of perspective,
where shadows are thoughtful

and all the boys look pretty,
where the culture scatters

like gloves in a flood
and the clarity of an orchard

means the stars are shining,
though they are not our stars,

Paul Hoover

where, splendid and sere,
poetry tells the most fantastic lies

but you like the slap of its hand,
where desire longs for perfection

and ecstasy is a boundary,
where children open trapdoors,

in their confidence ruthless,
in their cruelties kind,

where memory is a lost empire
and "heaven is a pigsty,"

where the loud nurse cries
in her butterfly pavilion,

and the mind of god
is filled with furniture

too weak to ever sit on,
where *authentic* has no language,

and nothing is more real
than blinking at a screen,

where the labor of planets turning
is felt in the roots of your hair,

where "formless" has no meaning
and the memoir *Our Blimp*

is the hit of the season,
where purchasing a rifle

is easier than sleeping,
where the local ironies

are usually sympathetic
despite the lost worlds

in an instant of refraction,
small displacements of meaning

original as justice
and just as unfair,

where clean and well-lit
are all you can remember,

where truth is approximation
and time the best disguise.

from VIRIDIAN (1997)

IN A SHADOW GATE

Because it has rained and the TV
is on, the world is not itself.
No setting, no plot, no stable

sense of others, yet the vaguest
scent of events absorbs or rather
emits the earthy smell of light.

The woman writes, as if in space:
The boy shines in the house.
The meaning of the sentence

arrives like a shroud or mouth.
North of her eyes, desireable objects
occupy a blank page of heaven.

Strangers inside leaves.
The country flat with light.
A thrilling yellow mattress.

The boy shines in the house.
Addicted to the field, its weight
and circumstance, the boy unwinds

like water. She goes into a stone.
The "soft" sound of water
as the rainy capital floats

on smoke and real regret.
The sounds of struggle and laundry;
dust in South Dakota; and the reckless

scatter of swimming pools down
the California coast. Erasing all
the windows, making the furniture

nervous, light finds its northern
edge and sweeps south like a ghost.
Because the TV is on and leaves

are wet with rain, light is weight
of meaning as stone is always song.
She writes containment's *it*.

The boy is *in* the house.
Distance is of a form all eyes
are *on*, beyond the meaning fence.

STATIONARY JOURNEY

In the dwarf gardens of thought,
the century is distant and pristine.
Day flowers on its altar of daylight, laundry,
dead sunsets, and dying farms; everything
flows back to its source, deep in mother bone.

At the outskirts of everyplace else,
the afternoon grows tall then leans back in its window.
Isadora's scarf catches in Sylvia's wheel.
The traffic is calm as a locked museum.
Silence wakes with red leaves on its lips.

Equidistant from everything, we survive
the collision of causality and April.
The tin eyes of fish turn as if in thought.
Page after page of rain.
The day consists of milk, tomato soup,
and vague coincidence.

You see it all through the cellophane tape
that straps you to a wall. The hurricane warning sounds;
the murder trial begins; a tendril finds a hole
in the scenery and enters with a shrug.
Leaves burn and rot within a cove of snow.
Voices rise, tier on tier, toward a shrunken noun.

Yet nothing overlooks heaven.
Like a hinge in space, it connects the past
with its future: plaining priests, out-of-focus farms,
primitive silhouettes. Apologies blur in the blood.

The stationary journey is concealed by falling snow.
The ashes are very soon.
In the flying pavilion history is,
hero and victim alike mouth astonishment
at the fresh world wrapped in rags.

RED LILIES

In their blue vase overlooking the window,
red lilies show little compassion
for this or any effort on behalf of their beauty.
But they seem to like the rain
falling onto a pond,
pocking and denting its surface.
As for the rain itself,
these aisles of trees are its avenues,
where shadows fall like smoke.
Murky and operatic, it seems to announce
October's and any central idea.
The stealth of grass, for instance.
An orange painted orange.
Or the tendency to believe in coherence
because a storm sweeps through
disguised as a revelation.
All this occurs not at the banquet of theory
but rather in your eyes which savor and anneal
the secret flowers of night intimate and ancient.
Indistinct as the weather
but precise as blaring horns,
red lilies make children pregnant
with old mythologies
like harmony and sense.
Therefore, I sit on the porch of November
with my usual violent associates,
wind, rain, sleet, and hail,
observing the livid scene
beyond that fading vase.
I seem to have encountered desire on the first day
it was open then lost my way
in the questions it always posed,
as trivial as red lilies and finally just as important.
To look at the sea without understanding,
to sense the gulls' stupidity
as they turn their ancient eyes,
suggests the end of a journey only recently begun.

I can feel its heavy approach,
the dead boots of expectation.
Yet there it stands at the door,
its hair wet with arrival, a smile on its private face,
asking to be admitted.

BASEBALL

When the world finally ends,
a baseball will be hovering over a diamond
somewhere in New Jersey:
a flash of flesh falling out of its clothes
and suddenly no one's there.
The baseball, singed and glowing,
drops to the ground again.
But let's back up twenty years or so.
It's the 1970s and the Oakland As
have 19th Century faces,
as if they'd stepped from a Balzac novel.
A dynasty of troublesome players
who like to fight and slide,
they've just won their third World Series
but trip on their long hair
and wear Edwardian clothes,
the messy but dressy look.
Back then, I'd lie in bed all day,
watching the Cubs and Watergate
on a black and white TV.
Then I'd get up, write some poems,
and pick the goldfish off the floor,
which liked to leap from its tank
because the kissing gouramis
would suck pink holes in its sides.
The poems were not about kissing
but had a violent side,
the way a man's gaze can be "violent,"
fixing you into an object
that, while it lacks a "lack,"
stands up like a fetish.
You feel your face go rubber,
as if your body were filling
with grief. Meanwhile, Reggie Jackson,
while not completely phallocentric,
did create a firm impression
as he stroked the ball for a homer.
Sometimes he flailed and fell,

but now he's out of ball.
Lefthandedness is a sinister
business, but in the major leagues
you want a few of these wizards
on first base or the mound.
Does "mound" have a sexual sound?
And what about "stick men"?
Baseball in the movies—
for instance, *Field of Dreams*—
is basically conservative,
says Pauline Kael and one agrees:
"Play ball" is the message,
the dream of male tradition
passing and to come. Besides,
those uniforms, so quasi-pseudo-
semi-demi-military in fashion!
They make us watch them swing
their sticks; slide between
another man's legs, as if
that torso heaven were all
the spit we're worth, we who
sit and dream, eat and talk,
as gulls stir over the field.
I like to watch the grass,
a simple wedge of astonishment
each time I enter the park.
Then the boffo noise of the crowd
clucks and drones like an engine.
I want a hot dog now! And beer
to spill down concrete steps.
My goodness, some of those guys
actually look like gods.
And some of them look just
upwardly mobile, tossing a wink
at their accountants Horvath,
Perkins, Wiggins, and Peal.
One imagines the Yankee Clipper,
smooth as smoke, crossing an outfield of fog.
Lou Gehrig stands at the mike,
saying an iron goodbye, and Babe Ruth

points at a fence where the ball
will probably go. Here's Pepper Martin
putting his spikes in your face,
Dizzy Dean's elegant rasp
as he chews a point with PeeWee Reese.
I remember when Cincinnatti
had Birdie Tebbitts, Dusty Rhodes,
Vada Pinson, and Ted Kluzewski.
The sponsor was Hudepohl beer,
and they played in Crosley Field.
The man sitting next to us
waved a gun whenever a run was scored,
then put it back in his girlfriend's
purse. We thought that was fine.
Claes Oldenburg insists that
baseball is an "aesthetic game,"
all that flutter of color
creating the eye when strict rows
randomly move. But "poetry in motion"?
I can't say I agree. Poetry
comes in your mouth like flesh.
It rises to the surface
like a ball held underwater,
bouncing a little but staying there,
hardly transcendental but present
nevertheless. You watch it watching you,
staying and going, the silk
suck of a curtain that seems
to leave the building by way
of a window one day, then slips
back over the sill because a door
was opened. Its absolute feet
aren't there, disappearing like
a corner the moment you approach.
Baseball, on the other hand,
presents itself like air,
love's green moment still,
at two in the afternoon.

Paul Hoover

VOICES OFF

"Into what language does the raised voice disappear?"
                                                    -Ralph Angel

A car drives over the mountain
with a pair of sunglasses at the hood's center.
The forgetful driver left them there
while strapping his kids in back.
Now they're asleep, and he's thinking
of music, the language of birds.
As John Lee Hooker sings "I'm in the Mood,"
"Crawling King Snake," and "Tupelo Blues,"
the glasses look out at the road
and sudden panels of sky within reach
of a tin ocean. With the clarity of light
grained and reticuled, solid as a statue
of some new god, the sunglasses receive
the pious fact of every sensation.
The driver listens to John Lee Hooker;
the highway's mica shines. Life blows by
on all six sides.
                          It is not high noon
of the last day of the millennium, from which
the century's darker creatures, flying out
of Francis Bacon, shrink as if from antiseptic.
It's just another day for children to sleep
as geckos stretch like hands on the hot
limestone edge of a mountain near the beach.
In a niche of rock and shade, the actual
is in danger because the stars can't see
through the growing trellis of brightness
and shrouds our thoughts in the late
American day from the monstrous and
the sacred. John Lee Hooker, too old
to move from his chair, listens to his own music
several miles from here. We can hear it,
too, stretching across the mountain
past expensive houses in the dimness of a car.

Darkness marvels at pines rife with eucalyptus;
it knows the story we can tell
our post-literate children as they die
in front of a talk show and rise
as what we are. In that pair of eyes
empty as a fence, absence finds the sky:
sunglasses for the sun. When the car arrives
for dinner, I discover the glasses
and hand them to the driver. He smiles
and puts them on. The movie of the event
is only words, but there you have it—
an ordinary day with its rustle of vegetation
thirsty for fire, two passing trucks.

NIGHT OF THE HUNTER

According to the theory,
Madonna erased Madonna Ciccone;
white men erased the Cherokee nation;
Serbs erase Muslims; black men erase
black men; and guns erase everyone else
as night erases day.
   Everything is erased
including the trace of history,
which, like a cartoon dog,
draws the trail with his nose
but erases it with his tail.
Half erasure, half wisdom,
history rocks in her chair like Lillian Gish
in *Night of the Hunter*, a shotgun
in her lap. She loves the black-frocked
stranger with LOVE and HATE
tattooed on his fingers, despite
his being white and crazy—the kind of person
children flee like insects from a fire.
After locking him in the barn,
history waits for the sheriff's siren
to wail out of some perfect future
where everything is revealed, everything forgiven.
As poetry thrives on a perfect indifference,
history grows from hate and love.
It's like taking a nature walk
in the outer blast zone, where,
hidden in his burrow, a single badger
drags to the surface the accidental seeds
that will reconstruct the green forest.
This leads to other life and later of course
murder. The fox must have its mouse;
the mouse has lice. I read the other day
that some of the early Germans inhabiting
this country were so pacifistic
they refused to raise a hand when
the Delaware warriors killed their wives

and children. It was god's will,
they said: *One must never kill.*
One of them, however, kept a loaded gun,
and when a Delaware tribesman
walked over a rise, he shot him
in the forehead. The pacifists banished
him forever, and that is history.
We do the best we can to keep
from being erased. But time and the moment
wear us down. We are here and gone,
a flicker on the screen brilliantly remembered.
Even as we speak, words change the shape
of our mouths, creating and erasing
the captions beneath our faces:
(1) most authentic (2) hurricane victim
(3) future engineer (4) politically correct.
Pure form is finally shapeless,
or words to that effect. In an age of private jargon,
one can always make the dead zebra stand.
At century's dead end or walking
into stars, what was done to us
was done with our consent and shines more fiercely
than we are allowed to remember.
In the entry to that place, a beaded purse
from Oklahoma is ripped from fragile hands.

DESIRE

"It is this stale language, closed by the immense pressure of
all the men who do not speak it, that he must continue to use."
                                                        —R. Barthes

Five inches from
such eyes
snow the size

of a sentence
falls, shudders down
like light.

Then the light
king fades
and poetry's corpse

on the sofa sits,
swelling toward
the door.

Clouds in transit
feather brains,
operatic with desire

yet temporal on
the whole,
like gasoline

and fire.
"Containably romantic,"
the eye strides

toward desire.
It wants to coincide
with incidental

things, making
distance rare.
Exchange or

substitution
makes metaphor
aesthetic crime

in realism's mind,
painting "real
if nonexistent"

landscapes in
the man.
Containing words

and other clutter,
the body's packed
in lime

beneath the author's
house.
Synthesis is

its merit,
the unity in
scatter

coming on
like trucks,
though meaning

shits on that.
Thought ought not
resemble

that which it
endorse?
Rupture loves

Paul Hoover

the difference.
On the other hand,
intimate conviction

leads to
certain actions
final as

the night.
I can touch
you now

in sequences
of light
and words record

this urge,
but Chinese students
burn the train

and history knows
the difference,
swaying like

a train.
Tyrants' shadows
in its windows

strike a blow
on poetry's nose,
as if the future

might remember
"accident's practical
connotations."

The night
is blind
with tyrants.

THE GERMAN VERSION

Like acoustical
landmarks

hidden in
cathedrals

whose monumental
shadows

explore the name
of cave

in the very
temple of heaven,

memory, self,
and song

extinguish
the voice of Ishi

whose knife and
violin

like multitudes
of horns

minus waxen brass
transmit a

video history
inside machinery's

feather
since joy

is the father
of reading

heavy breathing
great applause

The marches can be
stopped

but this is not
desired

a chorus of boys
with fevers

an ode to the very
tense

inspired by drapes
of polyphonic

in a silence
disabused

The opening moment
is riven

or having arrived
it listens

Pauline dreams
the faintest

engine
a simple sermon's

"disparate
glitter"

in structures of
intention

contingency's moral
stance

oracular as it
gets

the polyhedral
tent

Smetana
Im

or ain't
meaning

"I am clean"
By means of birds

he sees
the digital

mix
Im Frühling

whose deeply
many feel

since still
enormity leaks

to illustrate
a point

the quaint
lesson's

small talk
sharing an arrival

trivial
but in style

IMPOSSIBLE OBJECT

Erotic play
within closed
systems results
in wedge

and sphere,
a phallic
ball that
rolls downhill

through the
house of
Rosalind Krauss,
who dreams

its bumpy
passage across
stormlit fields.
Our primitive

hopes refreshed,
we drink
the blood
cup deeply

then past
intention's edge.
The limp
policeman faints.

Evening spreads
a summer
lady day
sang first

to woo
and chide

her child.
Conditions everywhere

glare. You
and I
are matter
extravagant as

anger. The
dear face
of a
desert where

the kind
present sleeps
on a
platform like

the night
in reason's
plain blue
suit. It

happened to
the group
between the
train and

destination, to
carry what
had fallen
too far

on feeling's
path. At
memory's edge,
the little

hedge of
breath where
voices mix
like moths.

Evenings on
the moon.
Science of
the found

where red
hair burns
on thresholds
and ashes

fall like
notes. In
a hat
and suit,

the given
hour comes
due, its
fevers and

sensations actual
as plants.
Its celebrated
calm includes

such thrusts
of sun
between the
pines and

night. Here
is sentiment's
ladder, a
thirst for

change and
patience, a
crucifix in
a coat.

Original gods
have vanished,
leaving order's
pope: shrieks

and cracks
of leather
then wooden
afternoons of

larch, road,
pier, rose.
The difference
has changed.

Yet the
facts remain,
sonorous as
snow. Found

on summer's
porch, the
torn coat
of winter

defines the
passing man
as the
intimate murder

happens, tireless
as desire.
Our snake
hearts stir.

Blue light
fills a
room where
ghosts of

roses bloom.
Among familiar
strangers, we
discover letters

torn open
like her
mouth. Erotic
as machinery,

stuck in
reason's throat,
objects impose
themselves on

every open
eye. But
we can
only watch

the sharp
hand open
as memory
renders useless

the present
moment's knife
writing blind
in space.

AS QUIETLY AS DISTANT

Under the century, under the text,
blood and shape outside a certain bar
where a casual cop discovers (urging from himself)
the singing beauty puzzle.
An actual town. Salty smell of a cry.
We smile at the century painted.
Desire in movement's place.

Memory shines on the face of the reader
heading down the chutes of disaster.
Memory lies in the margins of gardens,
outside its rhythm as language.

The monotone speech of disaster.
The rainy taste of the window
where memory falls to water.
In musty rooms, desire is a success.
The sun of heaven
deepens like a glacier.

The flexed muscle, the world,
the deepening rain transparent.
At the margin of disaster, she lives
in the movements of gardens but not in blood and place.
In the mother sense, memory yields
the hazards of a nightdress.

The nightdress is the said,
as if to suggest a similar world
where light bends over water.
At her least hesitation,
the memory of nameless gardens
where two boys play with a white mouse,
holding it like an egg.
Gulls sweep past what changes.

At the level of a cry,
the shining train desire.
Flesh is in the text.
In blood and even this window,
desire is a telescope
where the reader of poems can be constructed,
field by field, like a painting.

Let it run in the margin of gardens.
She places her head in heaven.
The blunted hours. Memory's indifference.

Her painted shadows offer compensation
for the hazards of these ruins:
the moving landscape and waiting trains
at the far end of those gardens.
A fine rain falls beyond the beauty puzzle.

The memory has falls,
hazards within the fragments.
Urgent lovely strange,
but not the only whole.
At the far end of the new sense,
memory has its gardens
where, unlike light,
the history of her impressions
shines on the century painting.

THE GARDEN

Shining like a
voice, the world
is coming near.

Reality's blue hair
rubs against the
weather, remnant freaks

of sun objective
as a ghost.
Consisting of debris,

the village bell
is caught on
video camera, where

the contemplative person's
eternally ruffled feathers
are smoothed by

wind and rain,
the damp hand
of nature creating

acts of meaning
the crying mouth
undoes. Pressed between

two mirrors, the
garden's spectacle grows
heroic and pathetic.

The poem as
"act of attention"
watches the wrong

parade: necessity in
a swoon. Traditional
as dust, the

world remains insane.
The scent of
rain and money

possesses our names
and thoughts: rhythmic
gait of monsters

beneath the hieroglyphs.
Stained with present
tense, the coming

world is near,
its wallpaper roses
giant in the

dark and literal
as disorder. Knocking
at the known.

from THE NOVEL (1990)

— 24 —

The author rose from her own conceptual system
more or less intact. Though the soul
of the sentence was altered, with epithets for names,
her voice was ancient as paper, durable as gold.
She studied eternity as if it were winter love.
ohne licht und leer. Mind's singular pleasure
careened in a fever. Thought provided
the luminous world: the furniture of the word,
a simple multiple beast.
Thinking altered nature like an exercise in style,
but *Hermit's Holiday, Ellen Bright,*
and *Moxie* got written anyway.
Poor Ellen Bright, daughter of orphans!
What catastrophic information will life
share with her now? The stolid Edgar Deems
must never touch her soul with antiseptic hands.
Beneath her pillow on Sedgefield Terrace,
she kept a diary of her desires—
to be in Foster's intellectual arms,
heating the room with their blood!
That father favored Deems, whose face resembled
an open Bible, was savage fortune enough,
but mother had been seen, sodden in a garden,
wearing Foster's coat! The vicar arrived
for tea and tennis, wearing Foster's trousers!
A high cliff in her heart began to crumble
and fall into the sea. Antoinette, her rival.
smiled her little smile beneath the lilac tree,
and the face of Deems appeared in the sky,
massively transparent. Ellen Bright did not
run into the house, leaving a wake of tears.

She defeated them all at tennis, spilled tea
on Antoinette, and appeared onstage with Foster
in the smashing play of the same title.
Their final kiss is for all to see,
all who care about love and courage.

The surface in plain sight
was of a use impossibly tender;
return to sender with these words.

The still arrival lingers
between an inch and danger.

Sometimes dull is full
on the hill between two snows.

Taut signals freshen the evening reading.
The overt nation continued being
since slaughter needed a house
with a burning home behind it.

A whispered lecture seeks
water's brilliant size.
Freight's straight signs
stare at pairs of eyes.

The author opened her mail.
The kindest words had not been written,
but soon they would be hers,
an empire of signs invested with power.
She could read the wind in grass,
see the heart of a spider held to the light.
The world was meaningful—
no sentence could alter that.
Das Kind ist älter jetzt.
Forgive the errors in this typing,
for I am eighty years old,
and my skill is somewhat impaired.
An intimate conspiracy,

range of tenor and answers.
The linguistic melodrama
is geared to outside speech—
du vent à bout de force—
composed of substantive nothings.
She was by, of, about, and at.
The sentence performed a phonic act.
The sky is blue, the earth is green.
I am sixteen. People treat me good,
but I treat them bad.
The power of prayer on hair.
I want to drive my new Corvair.
On top of a table, in the trunk of a truck,
while playing the violin,
while reading *Aspects of the Theory of Syntax*,
while counting the kinds of ambiguity,
planting a garden, applying for a job,
and brushing my curious teeth.
Sonatina burocratica by Erik Satie
was actually composed by me.
I could write *Finnegans Wake*
in about five minutes.
I sat on the face of T. S. Eliot
and squirmed my butt around
Characters named Cleat, Close, and Clew
and a lovely man named Harlem Desire.
The sound itself of sound as sound.
Quiescent separation
                          of word from page
The malingerer lingers
        legato
        staccato
a winter count of birds
I imagined I said
        turning on the phonogram
dancing in the syllabary
a face conveying England
        Take a knight for instance
shorn of any resemblance

Gentlemen Ladies
start your engines
assignable texts
and let the *Cours* begin
Mark Bright will understand
Mark Bright will know the answer
as Ellen darkly pondered
mad in the attic bleeding snow

Care's
pretty
empty
surface
wears
bright
this
earnest
face
whence
depths
are
overwrought.
Recited
names
(Glissade,
Begat,
Lament),
narrated,
juxtaposed,
remember
songs
we
sang,
hang
like
things
in
space,
the

visual
utterance
blurred.
Feasible
cultures,
"lively
quiet,
excited,
incensed,"
signal
maximal
tones.
Diary's
fictions'
illicit
dictions
utter
outer
worlds:
fatted
calf,
pastured
lambs,
feverish
orchids,
glamorous
grammar,
scintillant
minutes,
horses
scratched.
Words
rigid
in
the
chase
hit
closure
on

the
nose.
All
right,
OK,
you
win.
Omnipotent Mwindo.
Hard-hearted Hannah.
Heroic Apollo.
Courageous Tecumseh.
High trees.
Oft thought.
Tudor England.
Thomas Macaulay.
Ellen Foster.
Soft Water.
Table Tennis.
Sotto Voce.
White Christmas.
My Life.
Proximate Distance.

A white bear slides beneath the ice.
It first appeared in *Tristram Shandy,* Chapter XLIII:
"A white bear! Very well. Have I ever seen one?
Might I ever have seen one? Am I ever to see one?
Ought I ever to have seen one? Or can I ever see one?"
Reading of one, you have one.
The white body of words isn't a woman or man.
It's a shape that carries them both,
shaking like meat, insolvent as water.
The author has stood at a thick glass panel,
watching a polar bear swim underwater,
its long legs gracefully striding.
The author has ridden a cow from Happy Valley
to Stormy Brook, the cow of patience and real events.
The author would mount a turtle, the turtle of elegance.
A black swan would appear to the writer,
beating its significant wings.
The sky was blue as a penguin's eye.
Talk of fever and teething.
People dead in another country
and Martians sending postcards home.
It was a time of resolution with no ending,
insistence with no beginning.
There was urgency and style, variation's blinking light,
and everything imagined piled in a seething heap.
Aide-Mémoire made sand blow into a shape.
The sound of a sentence came into the room,
gave a pathetic wave, and quietly went out of existence.
It was almost a song, nearly a speech after dinner,
alas on loan, amassed a fortune, amo, amas, amat.

To project my being there,
I sang a little song,
its furious blot of a heart
wrinkled like a plot.
They quickly gave the answer
to which I was the question.

They had prepared a "nor"
for the "never" we'd extended.
Ping Pong in the neighboring room
and Ping Chong on the phone.
Salesman asleep in sister's bed.
Striking yourself underwater
in a chilly little novel
yet to be written in Poland or France.
First kiss in Ocean Grove, naked lady
in the house next door. Killing the cat
with a .22 rifle. Norman Workman drowning.
Photo looking out of the album.
The abortion is now in Wisconsin.
The name of the town is Malta.
Just a quick note to let you know
I value the comments you made
at the symposium. Indeed, I will buy you lunch
and further discuss the matter.
If the man I'd killed was father,
who was this in my bed?
The bomb struck out in all directions,
passing through Swanee and Dave
on the way to the light beyond.
Lieutenant Gorge looked into the hole
that used to be their camp.
Only a pair of shoes remained,
filled with fucking blood.
Poetry is important fiction,
thought the dead marine.
An empty swimming pool
filled with the fucking neighbors.
Bob's dog's picture's great.
The flag didn't wave; it groaned,
tossing and retrieving its shadow.
Everything was the color of mud,
even the blood in his eye.
The only writer in any language
less exciting than Proust.
Robert Musil's philosophical music

turning to metal jelly.
Rising from the trench,
Gorge could see the sky.
When the second bullet came,
his body bucked and started,
then rocked back on its heels.
Lieutenant Gorge lay flat in mud,
against whose mothering
nothing stirred, a semblance
remembering buoyant water.
Things shaken in a hat.
Looking for stars up someone's sleeve.
The relative unimportance
of oppositional gestures,
regardless of the sonnet.
In the moribund ward,
masters of tastelessness
perform a Chinese fire drill.
The tacky sleaze of the soul's decor
could not be underscored.
We must take action against this sea of woes.
We must close the virulent houses
where torpid images writhe like water.
My mother is buried in Indiana,
low on a sloping hill.
My grandmother lies high in the dark,
by a river in Virginia.
The shadowy evidence photography provides.
Lost in the grain of being.

Some fabulous ascetic may suck the dust from heaven,
but for us, starry pieces of light freight
disrupt love and prize sight.
The classic poem of love and grief
takes the shape of theory
is what I mean to say.
Assertions' slight variations
build a pattern but never momentum,
synapses firing like rain.
A neon/garbage/neon/garbage beautiful dream,
panoramic actual speech
rolled by in diorama.
We recommend the superb saganaki
for its mildness and crispness.
The pastitsio, however, was not up
to expectation. Here at *Gourmand*,
where delightful palates meet delectable plates.
As the lights dimmed for roulade of beef,
my fascination with darkness,
with its morbid parallels in childhood,
incited a silence that ran
through the corridors thinking my name.
My youthful confidence was perhaps
a self-deception, born of picaresque
improvisation within the lyric waters
stirred by these very intentions.
A circle of mirrors distracted the eye,
dark hints mixed with OF and IF.
Because the governess sat on my lap?
      O, fie! the shaven thigh,
        Her cyan eye,
which weakened the moonlight's transcendence.
You better fucking believe it.
Let's do a conference call on this.
I take no pleasure
in the world's coherence.
Why did you think I did?

A strophe bleeds for formal snow
that eyes might understand.
But then who else is here,
wearing the usual prayers?
A souvenir pantoum fattens one to thinness.
Stick a pin in the map, and that's
where you begin, like eyes that open the moment of love.
Overtones agree. Amnesia dreams,
down to   a drill
point's   heat.
Those of us who lived with Elvis
could read him like a book.
All he had to say was "Gene,"
and Gene knew what he meant.
We did what he wanted
before he knew what it was.
Us girls at Graceland used to say
that the sight of phallic presence
obstructed our view of the feminine world.
He swept the room with a castrating look,
and the "privileged signifier"
fell from space-as-text.
To cut, cancel, paste, exchange, find,
relay, return, shift, exit, enter, print, and stop.
Inseminate incision; invaginate mimesis;
violate the fragment; engage in the annulment.
Because while we were reading,
the page was like a window
in which we saw ourselves as seers.
A palimpsest of memory written over life.
Genealogies, chronicles, duplicates,
notes, lists, tales, accounts,
copies, citations, archives, inventories,
monuments, reproductions, simulacra, fakes.
A subtle excess of truth. Mimed models'
mired measure mows moist meadow.
Received ideas like "anything goes."
        Necessary fiction
practices fragmentation, then

we enter the ruined museum.
Sooner or later the vibrant picture
turns around, embarrassed
because it wants to embrace you.
And you're in love with it, too.
A voice trembles in saying this,
because an afternoon nap
put its hand in morning's lap.
The rhymes are slant; the visual echo fades;
one practices, lately, consternation.
Branching down the page,
tree feels no constraint.
I reach for my bloody mirror,
wherein I stare at eyes
excised on a plane in space.
In the nonlandscape, nonarchitecture.
On the nonstage, the nonsituation.
Let leaping lizards lie. The lips
of myth no longer fit. His mind
was in a haze, a cloud that drifts
between a church and boiling water.
A running fox where a woman stood.
The daughter wore a red hood.
Largeness, shrewdness, benignity, joy.
Handsome daughters and milky sons.
Jet exhaust on pale blue skies.
In the name of the Father, Son,
and Holy Ghost. Walking downstairs,
over your head, into water.
It doesn't happen overnight,
and then it doesn't happen at all.
Ambivalence; Anxiety; Appetite;
Apprehension; Army; Art.
Begins with surrender of erotic power
to the genitals themselves.
To Build a Fire, an ode by Keats,
Tinker's Creek, Firing Line.
The writer as precise describer
finds his subject ripe: the shirt-

sleeved evangelist, gentians dirtied
by sunlight, weak sway of the sea
beneath a leaking boat.
All my staff can rest today—
needless our machinery!
Misty vale and mountain gray,
that is all the scenery.
If mankind dreamt collectively.

from IDEA (1987)

LONG HISTORY OF THE SHORT POEM

She dreamed they lived in Africa,
on a beautiful green savannah,
where they raised speckled apples
and owned a bright blue ladder.
Life was good and they were happy.
The following day, she knew,
they had to go on a trip
to buy some beautiful dirt,
the most beautiful dirt in the world!

This was a dream about money.

He dreamed he was lost in space,
floating around in a silver capsule,
and the name on his suit was Geezer.
Maybe he was old, the Geezer in Space or something.
He couldn't tell, since there wasn't a mirror,
just lots of fuzzy chrome.
All he could see was the tip of his nose,
which looked about the same.
The odd thing was, this music kept playing,
a black polka band or a white reggae group—
he couldn't tell the difference.
He also remembered thinking,
as he looked toward Saturn,
"If only I had a sister,
there would be nothing to fear."

This was a dream about courage.

She dreamed they owned an aquarium,
but in order to make it work
they had to put quarters in it,
like a Vibra-bed or TV set.
After they put one in,
the fish started moving again,
the water lights came on,
and the little mill in the corner,
with its plastic man in the doorway,
began to turn its wheel.

It was then, of course, they knew she was pregnant.

COMPARED TO WHAT

Here in California, where ants are crawling
all over my hand and trees are green for a reason
but I can't remember what, something flew into
Marsha's garden, hung strangely in the air
without apparently moving its wings. A death's

head moth, I think she said, but there for a while
it was the emanation of something otherworldly
like in a Forties movie where Biblical things
occur—Lionel Barrymore seized by an apple tree
into middle heaven. I forget the name of the movie,

but he thrashed around for awhile, and that was
impressive enough. When a bead of water thrills
all over the skillet, nothing else needs to happen
and you've had it for the rest of the day.
Where do you think you're going, says the teacher

sharply, who do you think you are? Honestly,
says another, I should have thought you were better.
All those heavenly strangers seem so familiar now.
A camera focuses, darkly, a river, with little
light suggestions, and the rest is fluorescent

New Jersey, where, singing into a bullhorn,
we achieve the lyrical moment, see the face
of Jesus Christ inside a bowl of Jello. It's like
when you stand in the grocery store and all
the specials are on, but no one's in the world.

Such is the state of metaphysics, late in the new
decade. This is the lovely valley above the ugly one.
Life compressed in language, sights compelled by sounds.
As if I were blind to the world, all my whole life long,
and then it came rushing at me, time and time again.

Paul Hoover

TRIBAL ITEM

At the video store,
I ask for *Lacombe, Lucien,*
the one where a maddening killer stops in the woods
to stare at a leaf for five or six minutes.

"We don't have it," says the clerk,
"but how do you spell it, like comb?"

I spell it, including the comma,
with slightly French overtones.
Then I call Louis Malle
as she grows smaller, leaving through curtains.
I stand around smug for a while,
among the screens with their faces:
Orson Welles as a mean little boy,
Joseph Cotton with a bottle of aspirin,
and here comes the clerk again.

"No way," she says, impressed with my knowledge.
"How about *The Conformist* instead?"

"You mean the one with what's his name
playing the saxophone inside a bombed-out house?"
She knows I mean Gene Hackman.

"No, that's *The Conversation,*
Coppola's last good movie.
The Conformist is Bertolucci."
She turns and points at a TV screen
where Jean Louis Trintignant
looks dark and gloomy
in the back of a black sedan.

"This looks familiar," I say,
"but I can't remember what happens next."
Each successive scene comes like a deja-vu:
"Oh, yeah. Oh, yeah. Oh, yeah."

Now three women are singing "One Little Fitty"
while he walks around in a booth.
This is the part, you can tell,
where he makes a pact with the devil:
"He becomes a Nazi, right?"

"It's the Fascists, not the Nazis," she says,
giving the ceiling a who–is–this look.

"That's what I meant," I insist.
"It's Italy in the Forties,
and Dominique Sanda loses her family."

"That was *The Garden of the Finzi-Continis.*"
Her smile, I see, is a wedge.

"Let me see . . . *The Conformist.*
Is this the one where he gets her in bed
while the family talks in the neighboring room?"

"That's the one," she says,
mouthing the words like I'm deaf,
"but it was her husband instead."
Now I'm shrinking like a train;
I'm very far away, but out of some tunnel I say,
"Oh, sure. *The Conformist.* I've seen it,"
and as she turns back to her work,
I stand among these video faces,
which show by their look of dark concern
how incredibly vain and foolish I am,
unlike Lucien Lacombe, who grew at least in his movie
from a killer of chickens to a starer at leaves.

THE ORPHANAGE FLORIST

At the Angel Guardian
Orphanage Florist, I saw
flowers blooming in the

middle of the winter,
five degrees below. They
troped against the window

in order to get
more light and wound
up frozen to it

(the window, not the
light). I also saw
a truck, blue against

the snow, on which
the name was written:
Angel Guardian Orphanage Florist.

It passes through the
streets as something totally
real. I'd thrill to

see it coming with
birds of paradise or
orchids for the prom

opening fertile petals, the
moist buds thrusting out.
Stevens said, "Death is

the mother of beauty."
I don't believe that
yet. A blue truck

on some snow, that
is the mother of
something, call it beauty

then. The neighborhood contains
the Midwest Mambo Club
and two stores named

Hosanna. The School of
Metaphysics used to be
located over Harry's Bar,

but now it's somewhere
else, behind an orange
door, some kind of

scam, no doubt. I'm
mental enough already, beetle
brow on fire with

momentary truth, grace to
stay alive, which takes
attention given. For seven

seconds once, I had
ambition fever, wanted to
be the thee, the

the for whom a
crowd would wait like
nervous mice, but that

was not the answer,
cancer of the heart.
"The Botticellian Trees" by

William Carlos Williams sends
its "ifs of color,"
delighting the very hair,

but word for word
for word, from glass
to light to flowers.

HEART OF DARKNESS

The flowers in the carpet the color
of blood remind me of the helmsman
in Conrad's famous story. He clutched
the spear as if he cherished it, and
his face toyed with a frown. It's
a beautiful tale about madness and
death, and I heartily recommend it
after you've finished *I Love Lucy,*
which images in its humor the loveliness
we feel. Then there was *The Life of
Riley*. Gillis, the next-door neighbor,
stood with William Bendix beneath a wing
at Boeing, riveting and gabbing. The
main theme seemed to be what sandwich
Babs had packed—not the sort of show
in which the mirror bleeds, no helmsman
on the floor. Add Pinky Lee to fifty
bucks and you get a million years
compact as dust on shelves. Backwards
we would say, "Sadness of note evokes,
returned has drollness and," but the
tether drops the bell in one of our
miscantations, and that's a speech
that fails beneath the skirt of thought.
The heart of darkness is a bull on fire
in a valley, giraffe lost in an alley.
Won't someone hire poor Pinky Lee?
He's dying to come back. But, no,
he just recedes like Kurtz's cry in
the jungle. While Marlow throws his
shoes in the river, Pinky stares at
a grey television which gives a little heat.

But make mine fascination. When I think
about the past, it's always in technical
French, and charts are spread in rooms
in the antique light of seeing. There's

an object on the table no one recognizes,
then a word is found for it, like Apache
lemonade. The dictionary says, "neglect
in reporting a crime." So I pass this
cogitation to you in object glass, and
you guess who I am through schemes of
"the" and "and." Extracted from blue
and desire, we both require a style
part obelisk, part reminder: to be
an O.B.E., a sterner obiter dictum.
Grim as chromosomes, we line up for
a cakewalk that leads to our division
into you and me. The world is stained
by gazes to which each thought adheres
like a pink tongue to a post, and the eye
rocks in its socket as it follows the
bouncing ball: thin, thin, thin. No
meaning overall, just a thing that
happened, the star boarder's frivolous
comments in a well-ferned anteroom
fictitious as horizons. (They recede
as we get nearer.) The whole exchange
revolves on a fondness for amusement.
Plants rise in their delight that something
stirred them up, and I pour myself on you
with modesty and restraint in spite of
an arrogant gift that frames you like
a portrait of Juan Benito Juarez, neither
man nor words. This means: I will kill
you. Then: Your brother will kill me.
When the silent actress lifts her face
to the light, it erases her Byzantine
features. Everyone stares at the sky
where the Paraclete parachutes, his thin
Einsteinian hair making an aura of words.

It reminds me of a dogfight above Danville,
Ohio. The planes got mixed together, and both
came blinking down. One pilot floated into

his own backyard, but the other was strapped
to his seat and landed face-first in a field.
We ran around with our hands in the air,
glad, almost, it happened, for those were
the days when people would run from their
houses to watch a jet go over: father with
half his mustache and a shaving mug in hand,
mother with a plate of liver she was going
to inflict on the kids. Isn't it odd, I used
to think, that everything has a name? That
jet could be "banana" for all the language
knows, and the back of the knee has a title
which means "a clear philosophical view."
Each word attends its picture then fades like
a painterly trait: the apple with its curves,
light that shines like baldness. The memoir
of a *thing* is given in the open, like the
sponge of Francis Ponge, and its character
grows to a bold seduction. Yellower by
the minute, the eye becomes the lemon
reflected on its surface, and in spite of
an imminent shrug, I'm with it in the effort.
Language is a strafing run in no particular
line, proceeding from A to B through every
other point, of which I may be one, hulking
light of mind erasing as it goes. "Declamatory
unison of the whole band"? My dear, it's
raining pianists and plastic bowling trophies
with small bent men on top. It's pretty
heroic, though, how they hold the ball
like Zeno's arrow between this point and that,
neither leaving nor arriving but just plain
gathering dust: the French, the horn,
the leave, the tree, the shore, the toast,
the knot, the seam, the telephone, and
window. Blue creates the air. Green
is rather convincing. We get back Bach
in splinters, and saying turns its head
like an agitated mantis that hears its prey

approaching—low cries among the singers
consisting of General Song and the Chinese
Gongsters, a canto interruptus. Wavering
folds a father flag where can't pretend
is heights, and I shoot the barest step
one-tenth of one percent, since up
is in that realm, clear to hear the sibyl
drink a fascinating hand. It's a Poulenc
glass landscape. Widened in a face, collapsing
in the frame, there's now and then some fun
they tend to put on bread. A B-flat cat
on rat arranges rightness twenty-six
times three. Storms Pound Coast.

Which brings us to our theme, bright as
Indianapolis in a wincing summer rain.
I'd like to tie it up with a neat little
bow of darkness, bring back bony Kurtz
with his loss of words at the end. Not
a man as much as a place, he's sane as
Jimmy Stewart giving a worried look whenever
someone hugs him. He confesses to rolling
apples to see which way they lurch. It
cures him every time the light shakes through
a parrot's cage, and a sumptuous run on drums
wavers thoughtlessly, each note a dazzling
subject with endless variations on what
had seemed a plan. He loves the Edward
R. Murrow slouch of a city street. Are
landscapes more than acts? The plain
is very plain. He may say he never, but then
he finds he has, repeatedly and with meaning.

SUNLIGHT IN VERMONT

for Joe Brainard

After the circus we talk in our sleep.
"What is it?" we say, "What is it?"
and I think I know what we see:

an elephant sitting on haunches
like a baby after its bath
(it teetered above us with watery eyes).

And then there was Cincinnati,
the ancient clown with no sense of humor
who juggled surprisingly well.

No one could stand to watch him
in the half-deserted tent,
but, after all, we came for the pathos of it,

and every now and then
something great would happen.
The albino wearing the Gorgeous George wig

spat kerosene onto a fire
and rubbed flames on his arms.
We cried out in amazement,

for he snatched doves from the air,
a true and actual magic.
It's a lumpishly handsome world—

no "poverty of words,"
just a loveable charlatan
installing a small elation

like the warmth on your cheek after slapping.
With a mist in your head like a valley,
you search for the verbal excitement at fights,

and this too is a circus,
the crummier the better,
where a dog with rhinoceros skin,

"believed to be from China,"
can be seen for fifty cents.
For just a little more,

you can ride the elephant
around a baseball field,
swaying like a planet.

(We both realize,
as glances are exchanged
between the show and crowd,

that you coerce these words
to pose a satisfaction.
Between a hand and understanding,

our conversation gathers
like moths on a TV screen,
its being only phrasing,

something misheard in *MacBeth*
that later turns the plot
toward pleasant dreams and ease.)

2

Every five minutes today,
I rushed into the weather
to photograph a cloud

brushing the top of a mountain,
but the cosmic view from the side of a hill,
where we're entrenched with books,

is depressing after a while,
too remote for the mind to hold,
and the lens reduces the land,

can't smell the piney air,
feel wind pushing trees together.
Placing the photos in rows,

like Monet's lily pads,
reveals an empty obsession.
Yet the plain thing is enough,

and even more than we wanted,
a frivolous climate of *what*.
No characters float through

with characteristic manners,
mouths twisted in a thought
that will later cause them awe.

Today, to fight the loneliness here
and refusal of friends to love us,
I read a hundred pages of *Finnegans Wake*

and perfectly understood it!
Then Terry called from Lincoln, Nebraska,
to say he is getting divorced.

No such problems here.
We fight and get it over,
as one frog swallows another.

Last night's thunderstorm,
which wakened us into a daze,
continues to amaze us,

the clarity and length of sound
as it stumbled across the valley
like something made of rubber.

So, on the whole, it's too dramatic here,
the mountains presenting even farms
as something to consider,

Platonic cows that float in air.
I'd thrill for a lawn, that is;
turn my back to the window

with its saw-toothed mountain chain.
If you want to know,
Finnegans Wake is a prose meditation

in which Joyce justifies himself
not to God but to Ireland,
and it ends with a gracious nod

to his poor defeated father.
Thus ends my book report,
as the shade itself approaches,

not for a life but the evening,
attractively paratactic
like Baby Tuckoo sneezing.

Asleep in his mansion?
A shape in his man chin?
A sheep in his mention. Engines.

3

The "geologic opera" of hills reposing
should be a thought of its own,
quick as a continent shifting.

Today we climbed up Smuggler's Notch
where roads disappear in granite.
Maxine was wearing heels, and people

on the trail stared at her in amazement.
We were dressed for the shopping center,
not for the wilds they thought they were in.

At the top we found a stagnant pond
dammed by forest rangers
to look like a beaver had done it,

and I thought of Walden Pond
where Thoreau lived by Emerson's grace
while his mother did his laundry.

I'm glad it's used for swimming,
proud of radios playing Boston rock and roll.
But who am I to say it?

I'm about as involved in the matter
as smoke from an orange candle;
the memory of that opinion

is momentary air of which I am a part,
then we disappear together.
Each triangular leaf points in its own direction,

in and out of the light where
paths calm down to "nothing,"
if by that we mean ferns

growing in sturdy patches
and moments of green water
implying other life.

They amount to a story
that's simple enough in structure
but hard to understand,

arriving in pieces of this, that, then
that make a fretful presence
in the vacancy of an eye.

Subdued by the tension of years
stretching back to town,
I'm Joyce's "binocular man"

at the wrong end of the lens,
since that makes objects dear.
In the intervening mirror

reflecting cloud or ground,
there's a carpentered emptiness
often confused with a forest.

Shapes wear out their meaning
like jokes told several times
("Spouse of the boarder, down lexicon way").

I often forget what day it is
as light sweeps over the porch
and a hawk shadow crosses the field

to settle within some trees:
Harrier, Kestrel, Merlin.
And the sound of wind disturbs me.

Time is compacted in it,
insistently changing its manner.
I prefer the thought that nothing changes,

but even the rotting log
seen from the kitchen window
is turning to mushrooms and bugs—

it gives me the shivers, frankly.
How can people sit, as we saw yesterday,
in a tent of mosquito netting

while the wind lurches walls around them
like Catherine Deneuve in *Repulsion*
walking a breathing hall

with a rabbit in her purse?
I could never understand it.
Of course, if you're writing a poem,

some mortal symbolism might be of help,
launching a wave that never breaks
in an ocean you've had to construct.

4

"Dear Sir: I hope you'll consider reading
my book called *Reading Treasures*.
It consists of original words not like any other,

plus feelings and fantasies
none of which are true.
I'm also including pictures

that should give you Bare Ideas!
Keep them if you wish,
and as they fade through time

I hope you'll think of me
when the ambulance stalls in mental traffic
and percussion, pressure, and force

collide with homogenous light
in the rushing field and ether.
You give me money then?

But consider centripetal forceps.
The velocity of an average man
escaping a burning house

creates its own conventions, not
from its arguments with the fire
but its quarrel with the language,

which like the water imprisoned in rock
will steam out during discussion
yet not deflate the rock.

Perhaps Siam strong man?
The whirled and all its charms?
Supposing the laws of inertia,

the exertion of a finger
sends the perfect cart
over the perfect road

through the wilderness of Jack Skelley,
and a list of flashbacks occurs
in roughly the order they happened.

I'm glad you apprehend.
Both pink and circumspect,
with a sense of deep predation,

we sail toward Neonism, Gee Odes,
and Schuylerites, high on the quartz content.
Terrif! But topical, just so topical!

Dressed in polyester, how many have you,
horses? I have jump and flat.
In what sense do you think

Seurat's *Grande Jatte* is knowledge?
It's very understood,
no new ledge where to stand,

but important if it awes
or simply frames us there,
a smirk without its gods:

one thousand illustrations.
I hope you like my meaning and soon
will punish it. Yours in the pen, etc."

5

Moths are covering windows,
though more sparsely than before.
I could turn out the lights

and watch them disappear,
but there's something appealing about them
as they strike the screen like fingers.

Today we saw the beaver pond
at the top of the hill,
its muddy lodge and sulfurous water.

Some call it Blueberry Hill,
both for the blueberries there
and for the lovers who visit,

but we weren't in that kind of mood.
The usual view was bluer, more fluorescent,
and none of us knew the names of trees,

so now I look through a book
containing Shadblows, Hawthorns,
and a kind of Prickly Ash

called the Toothache Tree.
It's the only northern citrus,
with berries that numb the palate,

and it often hosts the "orange dog,"
a caterpillar, which, when excited,
emits the odor of rotting lemons.

I also look up Poplar *(Populus Tremuloides).*
Yesterday, pointing at one I'd liked,
a neighbor called it "junk."

Paul Hoover

Farmers will cut them like weeds,
but known as Trembling Aspens,
with thin white bark and leaves

that flash like spoons,
they're useful to the tourist.
Says Donald Culross Peattie,

"A breeze that is barely felt on the cheek
will send the foliage into a panic whisper."
Most of the day I slept, upset

by something mean I'd said.
All sentiment is ambition,
or so I've recently thought,

plus getting older gives me the present
a sentence at a time.
Flushed with that "success,"

I commit to memory the same old darkness
for which the dead are justly famous.
Here the land is never flat

between two dwindling towns.
Rain shrugs toward coasts
years and rivers later.

6

In the early morning when Joe gets up,
two herons are on the pond
eating the small brown trout.

Maybe nothing in nature is clumsy
until the moment it dies,
and we can't help watching that,

though to gawk is not to see,
if I understand Confucius.
It's character that counts.

But let's not dwell in truth.
It's delightful all around us,
therefore also gone.

What are words to do
between a yes and yet?
They'll never change our lives,

so what did you expect?
And what did I think I wanted,
to be sadder and wiser, maybe?

On the other hand,
in the movie I watched last night
(*A Midsummer Night's Dream*),

Puck was played by Mickey Rooney
with hysteria and grandeur,
and Bottom was played by Cagney.

I loved their tragical mirth,
the ethereal voices
of tapdancing Maypole dancers

swirling in silk and darkness.
"Lead kindly, light"
is also a fine thing to hear

in the woods near a red farmhouse
with its family cemetery
exuding *memento mori*.

And so I go to sleep
in the midst of kindly nature,
my donkey head next to the princess.

7

I read today that Estée Lauder,
while having some ladies to tea,
made them stand on their heads in the garden

because they looked so sluggish,
and Magritte was so annoyed
when a stranger came to visit

he kicked him in the seat of his pants
then pretended nothing had happened.
When I feel anti-social,

I crawl into the carpet
with its memoir of spilled drinks,
so even when a lady places a card in my hand,

as she leaves with another man,
suggesting we meet by the sea,
I blush more from politeness

than from any lust I feel.
After a while, of course,
shyness loses its strict insistence

like an officer under fire,
and something like desperation
waves its little flag.

I mean, I think, what I'm saying.
Episodes pile up that will only embarrass me later
with breezy digressions in doubtful taste,

but at least the window is open—
you can turn your car that way,
where civility is a bird announcing

how far its authority stretches.
Each new speculation is the story of self
both expansive and compressed.

You pretty well know the rest,
the "politesse de Durwood Kirby"
that is ours and ours alone.

So when ideas "happen,"
there's always a tent to pitch
on the windy slope of a notion.

As I wrote for Kenward today,
Bill's work is fully lighted
by the mind with its memory pressures

and by the "continuous present"
of the world outside the eye.
The dominoes fall in circles

with the clicking rush of tongues.
Feelings arrive as they will,
lived as they are imagined.

Refreshed from the rain-shaped pond
where a brat tossed a toad in the water
to see if it would float and the reeds

along the edge frightened everyone,
I begin to feel a lightness
running through my hands.

It's good you see right through me,
like the spoon in a glass of water
that bends toward the back of your head.

Each side of that amazement,
we're lover and fanatic,
having the same intentions

but different means and ends,
what was once remembered
and what remains to be seen.

from NERVOUS SONGS (1986)

MEYER IS A BUM

Perfection is an old heartache, the lasting
imbalance when two equal opposites meet.
Perfection makes an arch like a song,
ascending to passiveness from brute force.
When the singer is imperfect, a sailor
beating with oars, the song does not proceed,
turns in circles, sinks. Eccentric wheels,
irregular as pears, move powerfully as verbs,

but Meyer with his perfect daughters, Meyer
is a bum. He floats like an angel in his tub.
The voices in a choir sound awful one at a time,
magnificent together. Meyer is singing along,
happy to find the world enlarged (it's smaller).
Perfection is a car to drive. Meyer is a bum.

BY THEIR LOVE ARE GROWN COSMOGRAPHERS

With boldness beneath your reserve, you're
like Canadian summer, the scent of glaciers
never distant (they sit like single minds).
You're shy as ice, shrill as a violin.
You travel passively by piano, describing
the world as it is: cosmeticians, cosmologists,
lettuce and silks of Cos, the meticulous corpse
you hope to be, dressed like an admiral.

Among the dread museums, monastic dualisms,
and drawings of Keats in a new crew-cut,
you sit on the laps of statues like a little
millionaire: Shakespeare, Goethe, Emily Ware,
The Great Houdini, Jack the Ripper, Uncle Horace
and Wilbur de Paris, stroking their marble hair.

IT NEVER EXISTED. IT REMAINS

One short millennial glance makes shade
like an apple tree with a bullet in it,
and the mind is a blue bedroom where
Lawrence Welk is on TV, inspiring you to say,
"I am, therefore I think." Total acne league.
Here in the North Country, hail is the size
of ladies' hats, hail is the size of Tennessee,
and "the right kind of riot" means you read

Readers' Digest every day. Your conscience & you agree
like a gospel preacher and his new shotgun: Something
must be done: Beauty comes in pairs: Sermons come
like rain and prayers are trucks on flatland roads.
In a thousand towns, statues from the Civil War
stand in the strychnine blue above their lists of names.

CLEM'S FARM

You don't know what to do there, what
where it is, or what you'll say to those
already there: ducks, pigs. You must applaud
the sun going down, stand on rural grass
discoursing with a cow, the two of you
like Hamlet and Ophelia, and it's the cow
tormented by indecision. Now you realize
it *is* an anxious god, next to which you're not,

those sad eyes, long mind, body of a maiden aunt,
like something made of paper, paint, saliva and
a kind expression. Among the flies and shit,
you talk to it convincingly: "O, stay with me
at Clem's Farm," but it remains the cow idea, complex
as a beard of bees, with legs like Carol Channing's.

IN A SUBURB OF THE SPIRIT

Everything has happened. Nothing is quite new.
Summer is so old it wrinkles at the edges.
Nothing is surprising. Nothing should alarm.
It's the same old rain over and over.
The sun is old, and the light is so decrepit
it lies flat on the ground and can't get up again.
Even your anger is old. It's large or small,
but all of your life it's been the same. Then

everything is new. Nothing ever ages. There
was no wind until just now, no glacier until you
thought of it. Fish change every second. Every glance
makes a new landscape, and the sea has a stiff new shine
as it moves around on crutches. Clouds are shaped
like typewriters. Things amaze. Nothing dies.

THE SCHOOL FOR OBJECTS

The world begins with rough and smooth,
stone in mouth, spool in hand, their
difference in a dream, and how you differ
touching them, formless as the weather.
They wince to a single mood, are impotent
to speak in states of always being, deep
from edge to edge. Their anecdote's inert,
a calm voice saying calmer things.

Nothing happens, then it happens again,
like mica flecks on metal that make the building
shine. Call it ordinary brilliance.
A stone is not a spool, nor are "two stones
each other's monument." They're shifting
monuments, take no risks, are true.

TRUMPET VOLUNTARY

Like pianos advancing on ice, each moment's
slow enough. The later years are agile,
leaping in with a razor, angry about something.
What do objects think? They're thinking you in bed,
cope with your delight, and yet a graver solitude
does not exist in Hor Zagreb or Paris.
An eye in a blue fishbowl, you imitate the room.
Each song's unsigned, sideways and unsteady,

and while the neighborhood is pleasant
with its silly eternal flame and women embracing
on trains, you hover like a change of subject.
Call it dangling conversation, but dangling from what?
In a desert tent an 8 x 10 hangs from canvas walls.
It's the president of the country, scowling.

GO INTO YOUR HOMES

Accidents can happen. Suppose a house
is blown together in a lumberyard explosion.
The perfect windows open, curtains take the breeze,
and portraits of your friends hang evenly on walls.
The blunt event is acted out, not on.
Nothing is imagined: is. No thing is imagined.
The house just falls together, rare as thought
in a song. It balances—no foundation—

then collapses on closer inspection like a
childhood symphony played. A giant foot
breaks through the ceiling; the wind gets strong.
A thousand things can happen, and they're
terribly disappointing. But the house stands
for a moment, true as a toothache, whole.

GEOMETRIC PRESSURE

You leap in with a "this is me, mom" look,
and it spills like a wasted hour impossible
to measure in a complicated room. The dimmest
citizen shrinks, or so he's fond of thinking,
when love of afternoons creates unfolded France
in the gridded middle west two times more edge
than center, Tuesday, June 19. Lethargy discovers
the myth its eye requires contracted to a swimming,

precise as an incision. Accidents are effective;
you ain't seen nothin' yet. A serious fact collapses
in the background noise of a baseball game which
only you can witness as if through crazy glass
before the sign-off theme. A moveable idea
amounts to actual blood. We would see a sign.

Paul Hoover

SECRET AND A THEME

People change their minds in the matter
of consequence, but the sequence counts
and the events. Their hum, nerve's bend,
is a yellow car in rain, "virtuous in
imagination." No sleek world sorrow,
no healing power. One word, one word
and someone to connect—the gentleman's
talking business. The car simply passes;

one simply watches. The day is typical.
The word "broadcast" means scattering of seeds
over chosen ground. Will they luxuriate?
I myself am growing the chaos of a theory
involving a leg on a couch. A mouth intends;
the ear receives. I shouldn't have revealed it.

INTOLERANT CONVERSATION

I comfort this to tease a forcing habit
part sorrow of a wrecking size that summer
leans to prove thin shame. You have asked for
cake, so naturally it follows men walk
on shining tables, boys stand in boats.
Assorted things like battered hats assume
a shadow address. To look the minimum,
I am more enacted to loll from it a name.

Follow and you will. The red da Vinci shoes
prepare the task of halftime yards outside
surviving you. A party shares the street
to shrug and look away. See the new amounts.
Blank as background noise, who had the courage
led three lives in the manner measuring weight.

INDUSTRIAL LAKE, INDIANA

Along the edge and deeper into the park,
couples lie in the shadows of cars they've shined
for the holiday. Then someone takes a picture
of trees reflected upside down, a few haphazard
bathers. It's the dullest possible landscape,
the colors faded and wrong, but someone he knows
is waving and a plane is going over; he takes
the stupid picture. Several years go by,

and a cousin once removed finds photos in the attic.
Now he also stands at the edge of a lake like trees,
feels the pleasure of their sameness collapsing
difference in a frame. Active wind moves actual water
along a shrugging line. Delaying light provides
the surface shine where poor dull gods exist.

BOSTON TO CHICAGO

You've learned the best part last, sensory
things half words: "though gentle not yet dull,
nor yet not flowering, full." It's spring
in lonesome, level middle states where flood
drill is conducted by men in yellow coats.
Flying over the harbor—as Olson said, "abiding"—
you see the decks of ships painted green as lawns,
a pleasant artifice in the hum of engines

taking you west: Sykesville, Kane, Oil City.
If a half-submerged TV floats down an avenue
that should be on the flag among those fifty stars.
In a bargain-brand empire, the horses have
beautiful names: Sinuous and Spellbound Prince.
The country's out of place: lots of land below.

AFTER MISS GRAVEN'S REMARKS

Boy, my left eye cries when I see kids
play violins and things. How did they get
so young? And I can't stop my fractures
when they strike toy xylophones in a song
too sentimental, mechanical sugarplum fairies.
It's brutal of them to kill me with growing up
like this, and Mrs. Pollen, who tends them,
why is she so kind under her matronly woolens?

What is so appealing in a clumsy, fuzzy
third-grader, ghostly in polyester as any
sad adult? Sure, there's no god to do it,
but they should have bright violent minds
to brace them for a while, and one tough look
keep them when Christmas isn't the mood.

WE'VE DECIDED

I can be myself today, tall space ape
in a garden where other space apes play.
What a nice time this will be! and I
can roll on the sides of my balled feet
like a hairy barrel loaded, swinging arms
that scratch the ground like leaves. I'm
an ape today, headed for my pulpit of joy
in sunshine by the window. Daughter laughs.

That's good. We can hear her mother dressing:
conspicuous absent rustle, dry nylon and hair.
Oh, lord of the spinal chord, what stone
repose do I feel when high heels spike
the spilled roast beef? I do not play
no rock and roll. I am an ape today.

AT THE MUSIC BOX

I am watching a movie in a theater
like a castle: parapets to the sides,
false sky overhead including blinking
stars, and the twisted faces of minor gods
gazing into the darkened crowd from
enormous samovars inscribed with sayings
from Horace. On screen, an ancient print
of *Wuthering Heights* barely smothers light.
Even the shadows gleam at the edge; then,
to my delight, the projectionist's giant
hand removes a nest of lint and dust
that had gathered on the lens. What is
Heathcliff doing, mucking about in the
heather, filling his arms with Kathy?
On velvet stairs, she proclaims her love
in spite of the dirt on his hands. It turns
to blood, of course, and he runs into
the storm past peacocks on the lawn
which shiver under their glitter. We are
a camera now, hiding behind a tree while
a party's going on: bright happiness
of the rich. One timid kiss from David Niven
won't change Kathy's mind, but his lands
and money will. Then Heathcliff gets
revenge. What tragedy will happen, what
violent love forsooth? Kathy dies
at the window while silly Heathcliff
holds her, then two ghosts holding hands
walk into the sunset like all the movies
then: Glenn Ford in the Army, Bill Holden
flying a plane, average guys who have to die
while their potent windows wait. O days
of wavy chenille hanging from Kansas
clotheslines! O tourist cabin with solemn
mattress and a trim little Coke machine
beneath the vacancy light in the Edward
Hopper night! Perhaps some family with

Paul Hoover

a Heathcliff daddy will stop in the 1950s
to watch stone crocodiles attempt to open
their jaws at a broken-down reptile farm
behind some orange signs in State of Rapture,
Georgia, but they drive on, easing farther
south with northern trepidation. Chain gangs
and mules are seen along the road. There's
a tinge of purple like underside of tongue
in the red soil of the fields designed by
Cecil DeMille, and the odor of magnolias
fills the car like a saxophone note decaying.
I am watching a movie at The Music Box
Theater on Southport Avenue. Stars blink
on the ceiling. "Only art endures,"
proclaims a samovar the size of Charlie Chan.

from SOMEBODY TALKS A LOT (1983)

POEMS WE CAN UNDERSTAND

If a monkey drives a car
down a colonnade facing the sea
and the palm trees to the left are tin
we don't understand it.

We want poems we can understand.
We want a god to lead us,
renaming the flowers and trees,
color-coding the scene,

doing bird calls for guests.
We want poems we can understand,
no sullen drunks making passes
next to an armadillo, no complex nothingness

amounting to a song,
no running in and out of walls
on the dry tongue of a mouse,
no bludgeoness, no girl, no sea that moves

with all deliberate speed, beside itself
and blue as water, inside itself and still,
no lizards on the table becoming absolute hands.
We want poetry we can understand,

the fingerprints on mother's dress,
pain of martyrs, scientists.
Please, no rabbit taking a rabbit
out of a yellow hat, no tattooed back

facing miles of desert, no wind.
We don't understand it.

Paul Hoover

THE CHINESE NOTEBOOK

Three summers ago, in Chinatown,
you bought the Chinese notebook,
Flying Eagle trademark,
with the flying eagle stamped in red
like an eye in the center of it.
Inside were gradual childish pages
gridded in lines that opened wide
like a city seen from the air.
It was respectable, calm.
The notebook sat unoccupied, and then one day
you sat down and occupied it
the way a gentleman enters an apple
or a cat walks through a wall,
with all due concern, with apologies.
And what if there were a place like this
(smokestacks, girders, noise)
where everything was smaller than life size,
though in proportion, innately good?
On the hazardous blue of the factory grass
you'd practice your nonchalant stroll
until you "got it right," and there was no need
for walking at all, just the thought of

ants contending   for the edge of a sleeve

and funny green lizards   eating the finches

of which there are two   in the world

Boats are slow   tangled in vines

Mr. Leopard   is the expert

er, um, uh, well   on the literature of

The face of the rock   did speak to him

saying you are tired   It is here we begin

---

our decent descent

departing day

wends his way

we climb, they climb

between two rhymes

the earth is green

from Park Nineteen

in the sea of the farm

a cold man flying

Electra lost

This is my ode

shaped like an ax

voices mere

Laughing Killer

Molly Bloom's

the truth is in

a bloodhound sniffing

as one who reads

I is another

Here is my heart

who sits in the house

O eloquent tourist

O Tennessee Ernie

as curfew tolls

the plowman homeward

I climb, you climb

the uneasy distance

The sky is blue

I am a driver

I think that I shall never see

the dream of hay

destroying a garden

the radios silent

to all the typos

my adolescence

across the aisle

Escapes from Jail

and yet, and yet

the joking aside

the edge of a nerve

only the margin

physical silver

placebo addict

thinking engines

high in a window

coup de tete

piles of ribbon

searching for you

a cold man flying

two tough Frenchmen

without the noble

confessing on buses

who roughly resemble

Lake Matapongpong

that dreamy village

from Kiss My Ass

until your word

Harold Bloom

first you 're conceived

please correct me

who speaks of the poet

Brasilia, Brazil

embroidered in carpets

and Liberace

a slow elevator

the war broke out

a mountain lion

writing verses

with terrible pleasure

build up on the floor

almost perfection

with stupid courage

beating a nun

nothing is simple

to total strangers

the book of the month

another Bing Crosby

where no one is born

to Something Or Other

is green again

surrounded by lions

then absent-minded

if I'm wrong

as "virgin hero"

you find your face

you that is

a wet painting on

that was the year

because I seen

now they've caught me

Emily moaned

reading an ode

to Wally Cox   or should that be

Hello out there!   the surgeon's face

when he has erred   the Shetland pony

Ernesto Cohen   the very blue

blue traffic cop   First Church of Sacred

Metaphysics   373-3289

This, too, the Chinese notebook knows,
as if in a windy mirror it could turn its pages
to drawings of cows and long simple lines
meaning rain. They slant off and go,
and a theory of art occurs,
that the melodies heard by peasants
through the open windows of the manor
are memorized by them
and sung again at their gatherings.
But the opposite also holds,
the aristocrat influenced
(he will say it came in a dream)
by evening songs from the cabins.
Eloquence either way,
and trimmed or untrimmed,
there's the beauty of the scenery,
the slow-moving, arthritic animals
that "decorate" the side of the road.
There's the sticky glass panel
separating you and the driver,
who now and then turns to face you
in a rage of speech and gestures.

HEART'S EASE

Near the curving harbor where pine trees father
there's the sense of a piece at a time within
the blurred eye of the whole, the sky a painted set
where joy is contemplating having no evident end.
A bog or swamp is hidden by the oblong lake

that stretches from state to state, pine needle paths
on ridges through neat sloughs imaging a heaven
of light and water fleas. Draw the bordering line
for which a blame is given. This plenitude exists.
A thinking is prepared as you pass long rows of trees

both sides of a window, and that is a way of saying.
A thinking is prepared for the reader who breaks
and enters. Lengthening narrows the series,
and I tend to open my mouth at the speed of such
a sum, revealing a new heroism where the system says

I AM, a scattered Adonis gathered. Fonder each time
dreamt, I had perjured myself in the Perry Como slippers
of rummaging through the snow. A shimmering chimera,
I had sat by a patterned wall amounting to a midden
while an image crossed the eye prior to the mind.

It rolled the center up, creating calm attention
from nothing like a mother. The hopeless spiritual
takes the name of rural, obliquely distancing,
heart's ease as a flower comforting by its name, that
dismayingly quiet child in that now crumbling town.

WORDS MY DAUGHTER ASKED FOR

Heaven is a city. St. Augustine thought so.
We'll live closely there, as bright and dull
as before. Growing into her beauty, my daughter
is a city kid. An only child, she is eagerness,
steady in her self, and a little attractively crazy.
She knows how to live. Today she asked me to write
all the words I know, the way that we ask her,
and instead of Mom and Dad and dog and cat,
I put down the following list as far as I
could stand to, falling into quatrains, rhyme,
in spite of it or me:

sincerely
Albuquerque
lastingly
whole

album
albumen
septic
dole

Simonize
drivel
elbow
fool

enemy
alibi
chimney
chin

loquacious
outrageous
enmity
prayer

wholesomely
handsomely
orange
potato

thoughtbound
outland
mountainous
razor

ceremonial
salami
evilly
severally

perenially
probably
nobly
and able

Nostalgia for the sake of it, a brooding honesty,
or truth with its well-known frown? Perhaps it's better
after all to write down words I know without connecting them.
"His sophisticated flutter-tonguing is both dated
and somewhat prophetic." Such confident criticism
I heard on the radio, concerning an old jazz star.
"Dated and somewhat prophetic": the goal I'd like to achieve
in the flat land of a thought. I want to see and shout
so far it seems forever. But it doesn't last forever,
walls off or slips away, and there are trees
that decorate and obscure the passages of sight.
Of course it's better that way. I'd hate to think
I wasn't missing something. Every step I take
offers one new chapter in the sense of a different setting.
I might spend hours staring at a simple head of lettuce,
so off-green, so firm. There's a kind of empathy in it,
as much for it as for me. Confluence is the word,
singleness of mind like a knot in a noose in a drawer.
Necktie, that is, the weather of that condition,

and I confess that I am charmed by the fact
of deer crossings. They're the peacefullest places
on the whole highway, and for deer that can read
they work out pretty well. I certainly wanted to mention it,
as time is slipping away between delight and instruction.
So let's just leave it there, the opposite of grandeur,
what was politely on my mind or junketing through on holiday.

WRITTEN IN JUICE OF LEMON

On the table is the gift you fear opening, something about the
rubberish ribbon or subtle wrinkle along one side, or is it just
the shape of it, too angular or square, suspiciously squeaking?
(Disguised as assassins, the courtiers enter bearing jewels.) You
could take up scissors dancing, make jokes about Limburger
cheese, or write a treatise in praise of country life, for here,
dividing the air from its angels, the orange interview
concludes. You're blent with consolation into one reptilian
shell, five stones' throw from summer (*et comme Moïse éleva
le serpent dans le désert-c'est Moi, Moi qui efface tes
transgressions pour l'amour de Moi.*) It's the river of verbs you
cross at the same place at the same time every day, then the
shrewd slow-down of nouns makes a cloud around a clicking
machine. Things flower toward themselves, never quite
erupting with serious unseriousness. The same river, the same
time—there's a schedule.

It is often said that where there are
puzzling problems there are also drastic means. What demands
your attention, like statues placed in windows, gathers the
street with its eyes: a choir consisting of roses, rhubarb, sugar
and fish. Your awkward intimism shines, preserves, protects
and bewilders, a punctuation broken only by words. You
clumsily carve a complete ceremonious curve. Among such
gallant moments, the plain cloth coat routine serves with
boyishness and bouyancy; you soak into the fabric of it, down
to the last denials of a see-the-stars, water-through-the-sleeve
performance. Ping-pong in the morning, golf in the afternoon, a
walk around the one-inch lake—such is the daily rigor common
to those our size. But who will stand by the harbor, surprised at
all the water there is? Who will express the weight of the
world?

Fresh responses to earlier questions, the bright light
when the back is turned, a "false world, goodnight"
enthusiasm—all can turn to sudden violence, kicking at your
ears and eyes. Beyond the sign "Historic District," through the
massive entrance gates, there's nothing but a field. You know
you should lie down on it. The sky and trees are for you, and if

children fear your approach and cry at the sound of your name, you feel a reluctant pity, tyrant. Everything you see and are relics a past that never was, yet which you wish to resume, for the past will follow its crumbs back home from the place where it was periled. Death is green to the door, forgetful, goofy and balmy (and that in a British accent). The answer is: taking its toll. But there are many answers, each with its hundred questions. Wonderment increases. Blushing comfort bites its nails. You lean close to whisper conspiratorial nothings, an orchestra adrift with its tents and flags, for when the air is a vibrating engine, and waves come up like chairs, it's hard to say just what you mean. You mean, you think, a landscape of bottles, waste and churches. You mean the hand through the door of it, the lady swoons of it, the "q" in quaint and full farm which is the "of" of it, and the mind of the ocean slipping through it.

But it's more like a random purchase in a store. On the street you gracefully hold the object wrapped in tomorrow's paper, a thing for which you have no use and which *must never be displayed.* It seems a kind of clock, the hands resembling a woman's legs (you'd think she'd kick off her shoes). All of your life you've heard the same short song with two long notes, like a factory whistle or bird, and now the light rushes up, darkening the screen in places. This, it seems, bears watching.

SOMEBODY TALKS A LOT

You've left the back door open
because a storm is coming,
blue as a shoe and almost as silent.
You like to see it move the wheat,
the struggle of trucks on a hilly bend
which a glacier once shoved there.
Filled with toasters or pillows,
they make it to the city;
then the shadows of trucks,
lagging like a window, follow on their way:
Red Ball Express, Pacific Intermountain.
There's just one hill. The rest is flat,
and seasons fall down on the place.
Summer buzzes and idles;
the garden goes up with a bang.
Once you found a rock out there
worked to the surface by summer and winter,
and it was the tooth of a shark.
That's just how crazy it gets,
and sometimes in a strain
you can see right across the country:
greasewood deserts after a rain,
the tiled roofs of a town
where insomnia twitches its muscles.
Earth crumbs fall from rising plants
that darken as they age.
Rain falls that might cut glass—
a storm or truck is passing.
It's evening in the country.
If the book you're reading swells
or a leaf falls out like a blunt red hand,
a strand of hair should mark that page.
You're walking to the door.
Decisive quiet is there, solid as a man.
You don't run around scaring cats
or wink at clumsy birds in trees.
The casual ceremony

is something you blunder into—
because the door is open
and a little rain comes in,
because the country is so quiet
someone has to do the talking.

PIANO FOR EIGHTY-EIGHT HANDS

Forty-four men sit at the piano.
They play Satie today.
One is thick. One is high.
One is aching, and one is enraged.
One strikes the keys with his broad forehead.
One is modest. One is honest.
One is Delgado Pianissimo Jones.
One shakes a tree. One is freezing.
One pleads to be awakened.
One is shaving, simply shaving.
One is cattle patiently grazing.
One is a fact. One is hereinafter enacted.
One is generous, well-mannered, brave.
One is a surgeon from L.A.
One has several enemies.
One has three anxieties.
One absently poses. One eats roses.
One is single. One is many.
One tips at cemeteries.
Forty-four men sit at the piano.
They play "Sly Jibes" and "Sonic Taxes."
They play "Boulder Rolling Down a Mountain."
They play "So What?" and "Bad Painting."
They play "Rhinoceros in Venice,"
"Tons of Grain" and "Drown in It."
They play "Blushing" and "Dumbing."
They play "What It Is I Wanted to Say,"
and they play "Don't Know" and "Maybe."
Forty-four men sit at the piano.
One strikes the keys with his broad forehead.

from LETTER TO EINSTEIN BEGINNING DEAR ALBERT (1979)

THE NATURE POEM

Beavers are the cops of the pond.
They find a crossroad
somewhere at its center,
sit waiting behind
their own bushy bodies.
They also patrol the outer edges,
swimming strongly among
the million water fleas,
which are fruit for other plankton,
more pure light than meat,
their bodies brighter than windows.

I see it all on television.
For my nerves, I could use
whole evenings of plankton.
I'd sit staring.
Plankton comedy.
Plankton melodrama.
All the tears and laughter!
Swirling like laundry!

How about those water striders,
moving on molecules
neither water nor air. I like
their in-betweenness, the sense
of nature's indecision,
though in another sense
existence is vastly decisive.

Here is our friend the water beetle,
a dervish perfectly halved in water.
It sees above and below, just as,
with my bifocals on, I can read a magazine
and also see into heaven.
Water strider, water beetle—
Abbott and Costello.
Charming creatures!

Late summer:
much suitcasing on the pond,
the weather often chilly,
unease as in armies approaching.
Certain birds are said
to tear themselves in air
(I think I heard correctly).
Appetite becomes direction.

The leaves take on their true colors
for the first time, red and brown minerals
rising from the soil.
Here is a tree rooted deep in blue clay,
oh marvelous.

This is the bullfrog
becoming bullfrog,
legs emerging through gill slits
of a vanishing tadpole.
The eyes rise, the mouth widens.
The announcer says, "Metamorphosis
is an ancient and successful strategy."
In literature, too, I advise him.
I woke up one morning as Franz Kafka,
skinnier than before
but a better writer.

Back at the pond,
cold begins to heal the water.
It is winter, sunlight rare, the only heat

in beaver dens and plankton.
It is a good time for staying indoors
watching nature programs on television.
Here come the evil trapper
and his villainous dog.
We are glad when they are outwitted.

In spring the pond is full.
Rain is an opulent engine
cruising every surface,
and I feel like the driver.
We pass the little Swedish church
where the suicide sits praying.
We pass the little pond
surrounded by lights and cameras.
I lean over the steering wheel
with a look of great concentration
as something stirs the surface an instant
but then withdraws and does not reappear.

ON HISTORY

"The murderer came down the chimney,
committed the deed and disappeared. . . ."
And it was beautiful outside.
The beautiful snow was falling,
heaping itself in a clearing
where Anselm once kissed Clara.
The plowboy stops to ponder
his horse's shine and flicker
there in the warm stable.
It is good to be him, at such a time.
A castle will do for the scene,
maidens bending strangely at the knee,
leopard and deer together.
It is the only way we know how to draw them,
everything skewed, flat-faced, wan.
A formal silence: the painting is drying
on the line with the laundry.
One looks closely, as if history were really in it,
smoking elders assured in their power,
stupid-looking children.
Then something goes round in the head
like a hawk circling stuffed game,
a way also of conceiving events—
history as a bad painting
hanging on a clothesline.
The painter's children run around.
But consider also the murderer's tracks in the snow,
their perfect calmness and alignment
approaching the awful house, and how,
sometime later, they zig-zag crazily back
in no decided direction.

Designed by
Samuel Retsov

▲

Text: 11 pt Bembo
Titles: 12 pt Prospero

▲

acid-free paper

▲

Printed by
McNaughton & Gunn